FranklinCovey™

Loving Reminders™

to make kids laugh

**60 fun notes that
add laughter to a child's day**

Also available, *Loving Reminders for kids, Loving Reminders for couples, Loving Reminders teen to teen,* **and** *Loving Reminders for families.*

FranklinCovey.

Special Acknowledgments:

Conceived and developed by Cheryl Kerzner
Designed and illustrated by Kim Mann
Written by Sunny Larson

Children are like sponges: absorbing the world around them. Society today, with its increasing negative influences, can make quite an impact on them. Our children can also be affected by the stressful, time-stretched lifestyle most parents encounter as they yearn for more balance with their family.

With all the pressure and exhaustion from juggling so many roles and responsibilities, we can lose sight of how remarkable our children are. We can lose sight of how often children need to know we believe in them.

I am very certain that all of us as adults want to do so much more to affirm our young children than we often end up doing. We hope that *Loving Reminders* make it a little easier to keep focusing on what matters most. And with this edition's emphasis on fun, we hope you can add some laughter to the love you share with the children in your life.

 Stephen R. Covey

❂ Turn these pages into Loving Reminders.

• Simply remove a message from the book.

• Write in a personal good wish.

• Fold as shown.

• Seal with a sticker from the back of the book.

• Tuck your *Loving Reminder* in a clever spot.

Loving Reminders to
make kids laugh

coupon

Good for one performance by

_____

☐ story

☐ song

☐ dance

☐ other _____

(Please specify.)

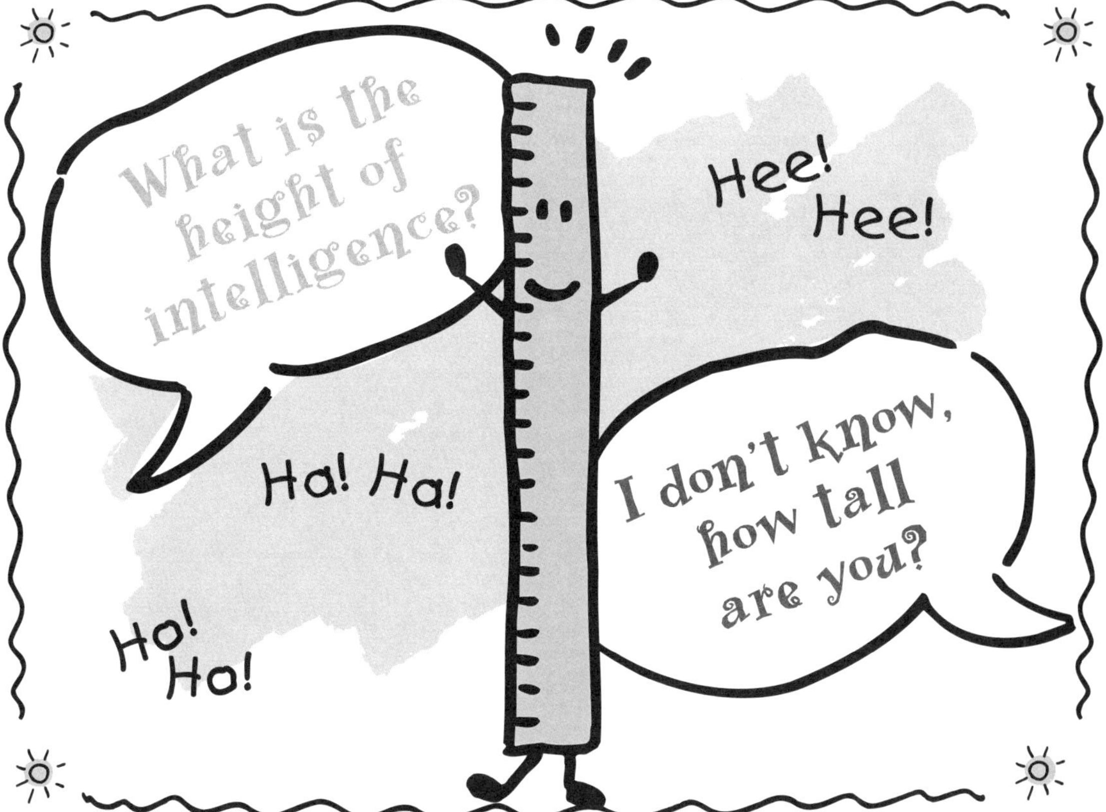

What is the height of intelligence?
Hee! Hee!
Ha! Ha!
I don't know, how tall are you?
Ho! Ho!

What do you get from a nervous cow?
Hee! Hee!
Milkshakes!
Ho! Ho!
Good luck on your test!
Ha! Ha!

Everything is a little more fun when you're around!

What's yellow and highly dangerous?
Ho! Ho!
Ha! Ha!
Shark infested banana pudding!
Hee! Hee!

Don't let
this slip
your mind:

_____

_____

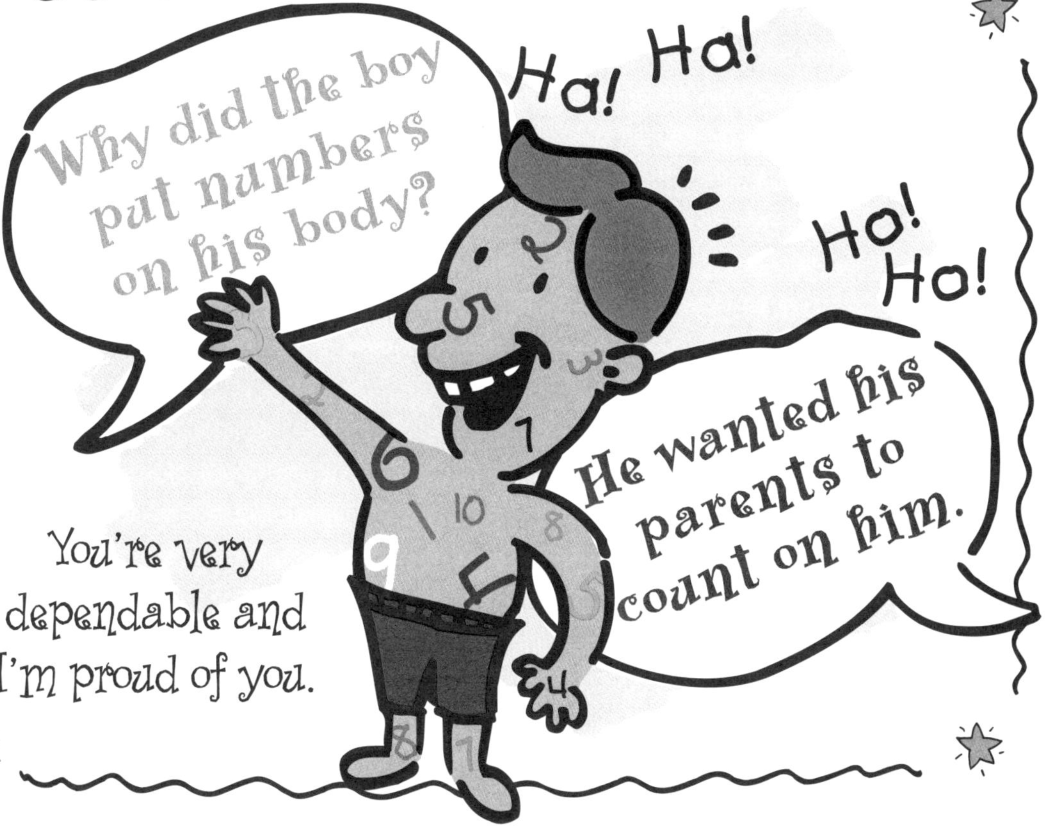

You're very dependable and I'm proud of you.

What is the height of intelligence?
Hee! Hee!
Ha! Ha!
Ho! Ho!
I don't know, how tall are you?

What do you get from a nervous cow?
Milkshakes!
Hee! Hee!
Ho! Ho!
Ha! Ha!
Good luck on your test!

What's yellow and highly dangerous?
Ho! Ho!
Ha! Ha!
Shark infested banana pudding!
Hee! Hee!

(I believe in you!)